Nora and Nell
A Paper Doll Coloring Book
Fashions From 1914
To Color, Cut, And Enjoy!

Kathleen Taylor

Instructions:

Color the pages with pens, crayons, colored pencils, or markers. If you are using markers, place a blank sheet of paper under your page, in case the markers bleed through.

Each outfit page comes with a "design your own prints" version, so you can do just that. Each
also has a fully embellished version for you to color, and a colored page, ready to cut.

**To make free-standing dolls, use a copier to print the uncolored page on card stock, or color the book page
and then use a glue stick to attach it to card stock before cutting.**

Enjoy!

**ISBN-13:
978-0692667699
ISBN-10:
0692667695**

Use a copier to print the dolls on card stock before coloring,

or color the dolls and then glue the page to card stock.

Nora

Fold

Fold

Use a copier to print the dolls on card stock before coloring,

or color the dolls and then glue the page to card stock.

Nell

Do not cut between arms and body

Fold   Fold

At Home

Design your own prints

At Home

Place tabs behind head

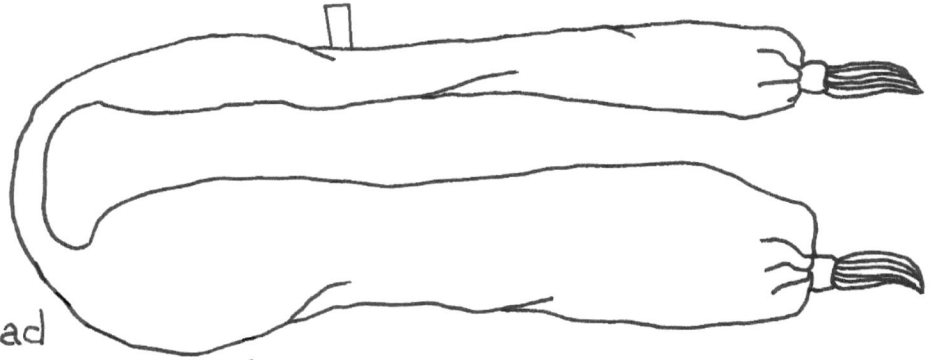

Design your own prints

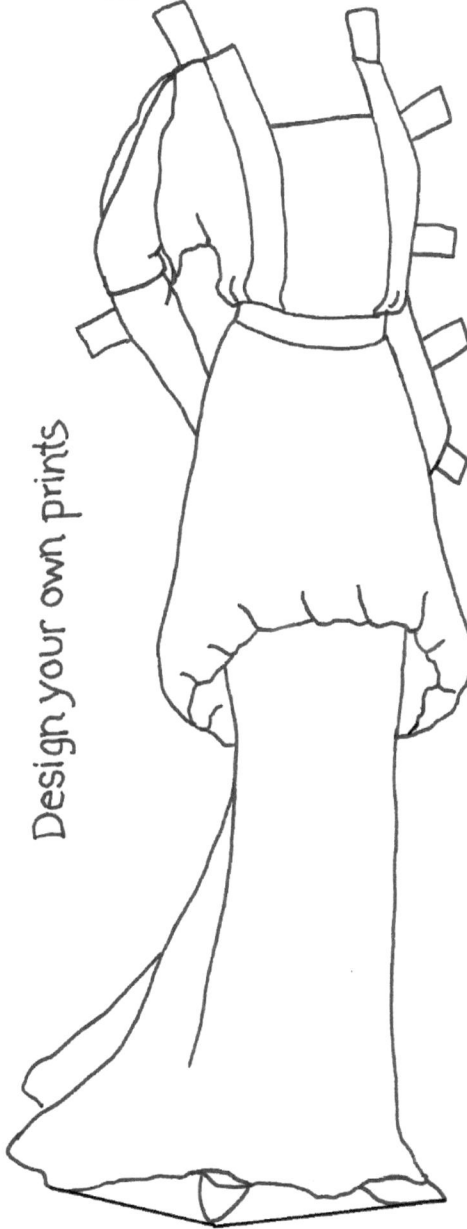

Evening Engagement

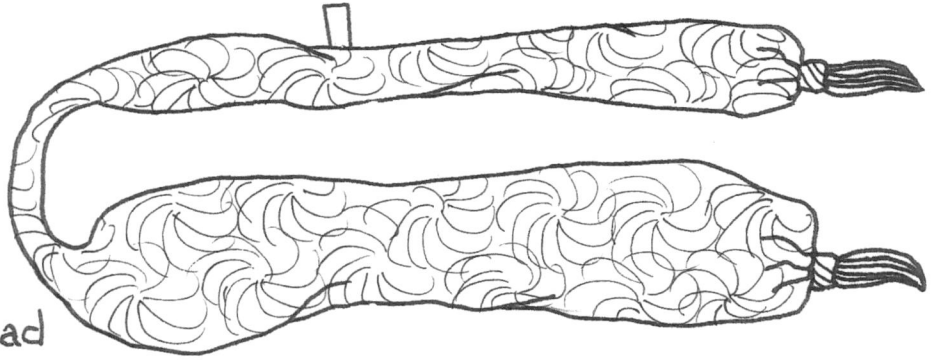

Place tabs behind head

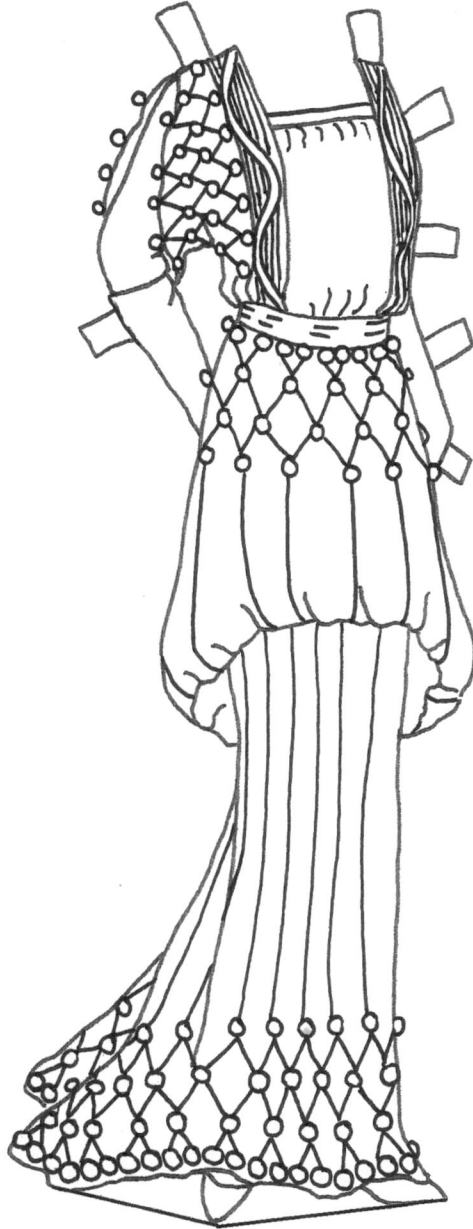

Evening Engagement

Healthful Activities

Design your own prints

Healthful Activities

Out and About

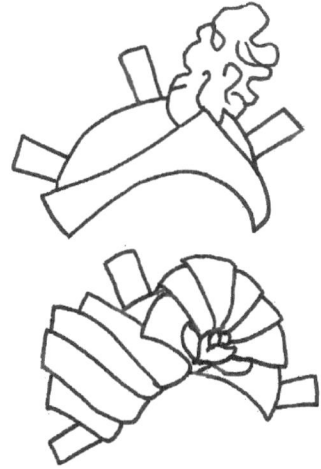

Design your own prints

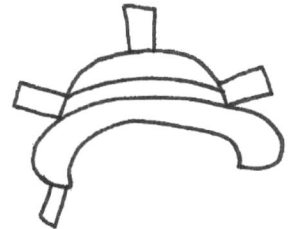

Note: Coats will not fit over all outfits

Out and About

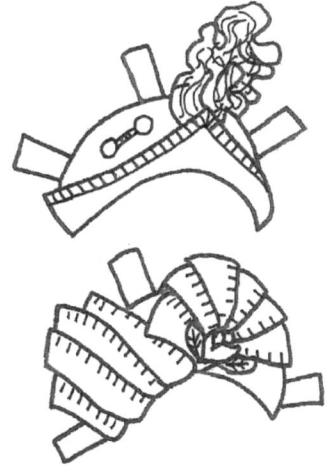

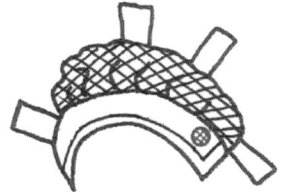

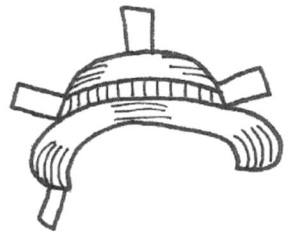

Note: Coats will not fit over all outfits

Design your own prints

School Time

School Time

Design your own prints

Sea Bathing

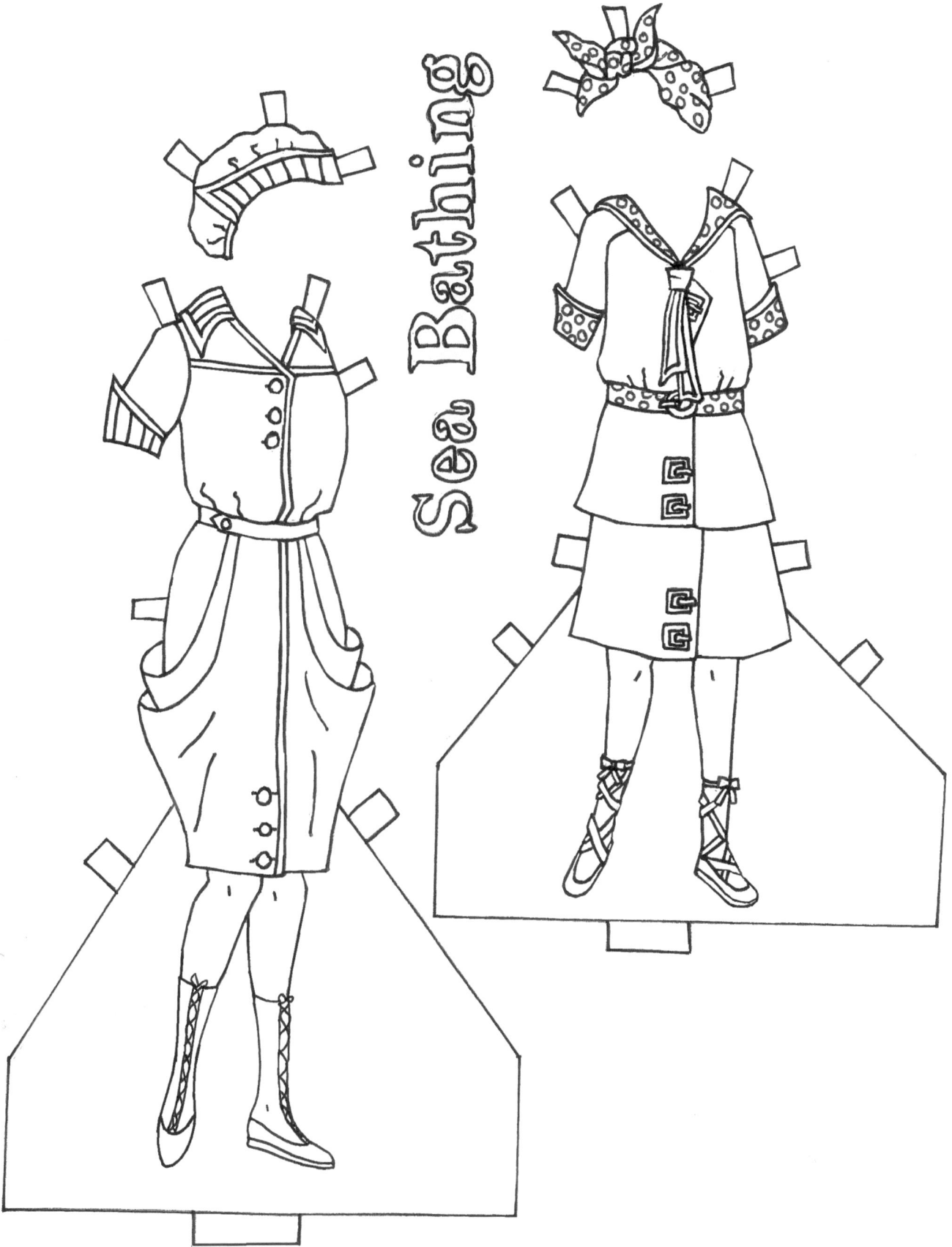

Sea Bathing

Mrs. Carmichael's Tea Party

Place tab behind head

Design your own prints

Place tab behind head

Mrs. Carmichael's Tea Party

At Home

Place tabs behind head

Evening Engagement

Healthful Activities

Out and About

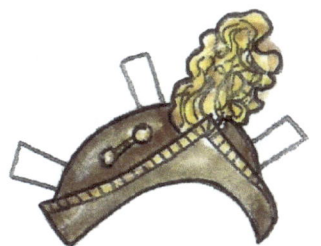

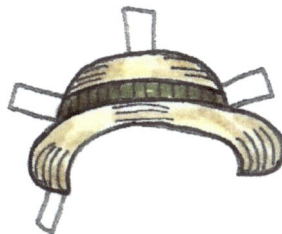

Note: Coats will not fit over all outfits

School Time

Sea Bathing

Place tab behind head

Mrs. Carmichael's Tea Party

Kathleen Taylor has been writing, designing, drawing, knitting, and spinning for most of her life. Her first magazine article was published in 1980, and since then she has written over 500 magazine articles, six mysteries, one mainstream novel, five knitting books,
and now, a series of paper doll coloring books.

Please share your colored pages on Instagram here: #ktpaperdoll and #ktcoloringbook
Keep up with what she's doing at Kathleen Taylor's Dakota Dreams blog
http://kathleen-dakotadreams.blogspot.com/

www.ingramcontent.com/pod-product-compliance
Lightning Source LLC
Chambersburg PA
CBHW041546040426
42447CB00002B/60

Kathleen Taylor, whose paper doll designs appeared in magazines in the '80s and early '90s, has taken up pen and pencil again, to design this set of dolls with fashions from 1914. With two dolls, seven pages of outfits to design, seven pages of outfits to color, and seven four-color pages to cut, paper doll lovers and coloring enthusiasts of all ages will find hours of entertainment here.

For free-standing dolls, either use a copier to print the uncolored dolls on card stock, or color the doll pages and then glue them to card stock before cutting.

Color, cut, and enjoy Nora and Nell, and their 1914 paper doll fashions!

ISBN 9780692667699

9 780692 667699

90000